Insomnia Diary

Pitt Poetry Series

Ed Ochester, Editor

Insomnia Diary

Bob Hicok

University of Pittsburgh Press

The publication of this book is supported by a grant
from the Pennsylvania Council on the Arts

Published by the University of Pittsburgh Press, Pittsburgh, Pa., 15260
Copyright © 2004, Bob Hicok
All rights reserved
Manufactured in the United States of America
Printed on acid-free paper
10 9 8 7 6 5 4 3 2 1
ISBN 0-8229-5842-2

For Eve

Contents

Insomnia Diary

Bottom of the ocean

At least once you should live with someone
more medicated than yourself. A tall man,
he closed his eyes before he spoke,
stocked groceries at night and heard voices.
We were eating cereal the first time,
Cream of Wheat. He said that she said
we're all out of evers without explaining
who she was or how many evers we had
to begin with or where they were kept.
I slept with an extra blanket that night.
This was strange but that year
I had to read Plato for a grade,
each circle's the bastard child
of a perfect O I remember he said,
and Kierkegaard I thought was writing stand-up
with *the self is a relation which relates*
itself to its own self but my roommate
nodded as I read this aloud, he'd stood
so long before carnival mirrors
that the idea of a face being a reflection
of a reflection of itself was common sense.
On the calendar the striptease of months,
dust quietly gathering on the shoulders
of older dust and because he'd not taken
the microwave apart and strapped its heart
to his head or talked to the 60-watt bulb
on the porch he thought he was better
and flushed his pills. Soon he was back
where windows are mesh and what's sharp
is banished and what can be thrown
is attached so unless you can lift

the whole building everyone is safe.
We had lunch a year later. Or
he spun the creamer and wore skin
made of glass while I ate a sandwich
and by that I mean I was hungry
and he was sealed in amber, a caul
of drugs meant to withstand ants and fire
nor did his mouth work but to hold words in.
I'd wanted to know all that time what happened
to our evers, to ask if he remembered
what he said and explain to him
he was an oracle that day, I wanted him
to tell me about the woman who whispered
or screamed that our chances were up
because the phrase had stayed in my life
as a command to survive myself.
That was the day I learned you can sit
with someone who's on the bottom
of the ocean and not get wet.
By the time he said things were good
he'd poured twelve sugars into a coffee
he never touched.

Small purchase

I drove my father for lettuce on the day his wife
didn't die but that was reasonably his fear.
His wife is my mother which has to be stated

if facts are what we're here to collect. I often
forget whole parts of my parents' lives
have nothing to do with me. We both watched

mountains of breath and pulse rise and fall
from left to right on the machine beside her bed,
only I didn't think of myself alone in a house

if those lines on the screen fell flat. In
the exhaustion of that image he walked to my car
through the potpourri of lilac and redbud,

shoulder-slumped but expressing gratitude
for the trees that make a seductress of air.
I took the stupid route if speed is valued

above history, that's my usual disease, the wish
to shave seconds from shortcut so I'll have
more time to worry about my need to slow down.

When we passed a ball field he told me a bat
cost 50 cents when he was a kid and that equaled
two lawns, of the wealthy sisters whose grassy

sea he mowed for ten years until he married, how
they called his mother even then, in their minds
he was ever the boy who pushed whispering blades.

Not long after that his father died and not long
after his father his brother died, whose
wordless body the nurses had tended for six years

like a garden. The day of each death
my father had to work he said as we entered
the store and made our way to the leafy heads,

no matter what happens you have to punch in
is the lesson I was meant to extract.
After searching the rack he found one head

hard enough, then to the cookies where everything
sweet was wrong, around the back of the store and up
to check out, where for 99 cents he became the owner

of one more thing that's mostly water. In the way
we touch by loosening up, I tried to shape sounds
around the nights that I look at my wife

asleep and think I'm hearing with every breath
her last, in the dark there's no quibbling
how readily the world shrugs us off.

We were in his drive by then and I was saying
splintered, was saying how unbearable, how clean
those moments are of the doubt about what I want,

what is right and what the difference is
between the two. To which he nodded and went
inside to make for one a simple green meal.

The semantics of flowers on Memorial Day

Historians will tell you my uncle
wouldn't have called it *World War II*
or the *Great War plus One* or *Tombstone*

over My Head. All of this language
came later. He and his buddies
knew it as *get my ass outta here*

or *fucking trench foot* and of course
sex please now. Petunias are an apology
for ignorance, my confidence

that saying *high-density bombing*
or *chunks of brain in cold coffee*
even suggests the athleticism

of his flinch or how casually
he picked the pieces out.
Geraniums symbolize the secrets

life kept from him, the wonder
of *variable-speed drill* and how
the sky would have changed had he lived

to shout *it's a girl.* My hands
enter dirt easily, a premonition.
I sit back on my uncle's stomach

exactly like I never did, he was
a picture to me, was my father
looking across a field at wheat

laying down to wind. For a while,
Tyrants' War and *War of World Freedom*
and *Anti-Nazi War* skirmished

for linguistic domination. If
my uncle called it anything
but *too many holes in too many bodies*

no flower can say. I plant marigolds
because they came cheap and who knows
what the earth's in the mood to eat.

Dropping the euphemism

He has five children, I'm papa
to a hundred pencils.
I bought the chair he sat in

from a book of chairs,
staplers and spikes
that let me play Vlad the Impaler

with invading memos. When I said
I have to lay you off
a parallel universe was born

in his face, one where flesh
is a loose shirt
taken to the river and beaten

against rocks. Just
by opening my mouth I destroyed
his faith he's a man

who can think *honey-glazed ham*
and act out the thought
with plastic or bills. We sat.

I stared at my hands, he stared
at the wall staring at my hands.
I said other things

about the excellent work he'd done
and the cycles of business
which are like

the roller-coaster thoughts
of an oscilloscope. All this time
I saw the eyes of his wife

which had always been brown
like almonds but were now brown
like the crust of bread. We walked

to the door, I shook his hand,
felt the bones pretending
to be strong. On his way home

there was a happy song
because de Sade invented radio,
the window was open, he saw

delphinium but couldn't remember
the name. I can only guess.
Maybe at each exit

that could have led his body
to Tempe, to Mars, he was tempted
to forget his basketball team

of sons, or that he ever liked
helping his wife clean carrots,
the silver sink turning orange.

Running's natural to most animals
who aren't part
of a lecture series on Nature's

Dead Ends. When I told him,
I saw he was looking for a place
in his brain to hide

his brain. I tried that later
with beer, it worked until I stood
at the toilet to make my little

waterfall, and thought of him
pushing back from a bar
to go make the same noise.

Calling him back from layoff

I called a man today. After he said
hello and I said hello came a pause
during which it would have been

confusing to say hello again so I said
how are you doing and guess what, he said
fine and wondered aloud how I was

and it turns out I'm OK. He
was on the couch watching cars
painted with ads for Budweiser follow cars

painted with ads for Tide around an oval
that's a metaphor for life because
most of us run out of gas and settle

for getting drunk in the stands
and shouting at someone in a t-shirt
we want kraut on our dog. I said

he could have his job back and during
the pause that followed his whiskers
scrubbed the mouthpiece clean

and his breath passed in and out
in the tidal fashion popular
with mammals until he broke through

with the words *how soon thank you
ohmyGod* which crossed his lips and drove
through the wires on the backs of ions

as one long word as one hard prayer
of relief meant to be heard
by the sky. When he began to cry I tried

with the shape of my silence to say
I understood but each confession
of fear and poverty was more awkward

than what you learn in the shower.
After he hung up I went outside and sat
with one hand in the bower of the other

and thought if I turn my head to the left
it changes the song of the oriole
and if I give a job to one stomach other

forks are naked and if tonight a steak
sizzles in his kitchen do the seven
other people staring at their phones

hear?

My life with a gardener

The screen door firecrackers closed.
I find her at the sundry drawer
prowling for twine. I'm nothing
she sees. There's a tornado
in her hair, her face is streaked
with dirt like markings applied
before the rituals of drums.
I've watched her shadow break free
and tend the next row of corn.
I understand this eagerness
as fully as I can speak for the ocean.
I say water is behind everything,
a blue dictator, say waves
are obsessed with their one word
but have no idea what that word is.
Her hands enter soil like needles
making the promise of a dress
from cloth. In December she begins
smelling lilacs, by February
she sees the holes
peppers burn through snow. I see her,
she's the last green thing I need.
When finally she's pushed inside
by the rude hands of dusk,
I set down my life for her skin,
taught all day how to smell
like the sun, and the hundred
directions of her hair, and eyes
that look through me to flowers
that only open their mouths
to speak with the moon.

Meeting Bill

Bill liked revealing his nipple ring
to new faces.
And telling the story of the tub,
the hundred dollars,
how as Bill
drew water the man's penis rose,
and the blade,
the penis nicked when the water
was just below the head,
how as one drop
of blood hit the water
the man came
and Bill left without words
or brush of skin.

He waited after the telling
for a deepening
of the listener's breath, a mouth
hung open.
And those guests
who noticed, who spoke
of the single drop of blood
as a subtle or delicate
measure,
or asked if the trick
smiled,
if the money was in an envelope
or spread on a table—
for them Bill opened a vial,
leaned close
and on the nail of his pinky

offered coke,
and only then
folded the herons of his kimono
across his chest,
revealing
the darker secret of his modesty.

An old story

It's hard being in love
with fireflies. I have to do
all the pots and pans.
When asked to parties
they always wear the same
color dress. I work days,
they punch in at dusk.
With the radio and a beer
I sit up doing bills,
jealous of men who've fallen
for the homebody stars.
When things are bad
they shake their asses
all over town, when good
my lips glow.

The documentary art

I watched Richard Nixon play piano for Jack Parr
forty years ago last night. Jack Parr smiled often

and moved like an octopus, the slow grace of one fluid
passing through another. The set was simple,

two chairs at an angle and one microphone on a stand,
curtains behind them to suggest a window and mountains

or an ocean beyond the curtain the eye could touch
if the curtains opened their mouth. Richard Nixon

was relaxed and spastic simultaneously,
and when he laughed it was like a dog wagging its tail.

I was breast-feeding, Kennedy was in the White House.
Richard Nixon moved to the piano to play a piece

he'd written. It was brutally romantic, lush
like drowning can be lush. While his right hand

was thinking his left hand watched. Reverse the same.
Only at the end did they work together, a studied

moment of detente between the halves of his brain.
The rest of the program showed Jack Parr in non–

Richard Nixon moments. Jack Parr in Kenya
with elephants. Jack Parr interviewing waves

with the keel of a boat. I kept thinking
of Richard Nixon working hard to make the air

sound beautiful and the bravery of his failure.
To be average before millions or worse,

to prove yourself just a bit above the curve
by making plunky sounds on a piano overdressed

in candelabra for the occasion. I'd whistle
the tune but can't remember how it went.

To inhabit its spirit go to the kitchen,

put the forlorn spoons in a bag and shake them

while biting your lip hard as you might
if the other kids wouldn't let you be president.

Becoming bird

It began with a gun to his back. Facedown,
he sniffed the skin of dead men
on an injection table the artist bought

for fifty from her cousin when the local
style of capital punishment regressed
from chemical to electrical. It was to be

one feather outside each scapula, an idea
that arrived while he flipped *Art
Through the Ages* past the side view

of *Kritios Boy*, who without arms and confined
to the appetite of marble, still seemed
poised for air, to lift through the roof

of the Acropolis Museum into the polluted sky
of Athens, bound for translucence. But healed,
turning left, right in a sandwich of mirrors,

the lonely feathers asked to be plucked,
the black ink grew from a root
of dusk to charcoal tip, they'd have fluttered

if wind arrived, reflex to join the rush,
but alone seemed less symbolic than forgotten.
So he returned to the Cunning Needle,

to Martha of pierced tongue and navel, said
wings and she slapped the table, added
coverts and scapulars, secondaries

and tertials, for a year needles chewed
his skin closer to hawk, to dove, injected
acrylic through tiny pearls of blood.

Then with a back that belonged to the sky
he couldn't stop, sprouted feathers
to collarline, down thighs, past knees

and his feet became scaled, claws gripped
the tops of his toes, she turned him over
for the fine work of down, he laid, arms

on the syringe-wings of the table,
a model of crucifixion dreaming flight
through the pricks. So now, by day's end

he can barely hold back the confidence
of his wings. At home, naked with eyes
closed, he feels wind as music

and dreams his body toward a mouse
skimming the woven grass, not considering
but inhabiting the attack, falling hard

as hunger teasing the reach of land,
while from the ink of the first tattoo
a real feather grows, useless but patient.

Another awkward stage of convalescence

Drunk, I kissed the moon
where it stretched on the floor.
I'd removed happiness from a green bottle,
both sipped and gulped
just as a river changes its mind,
mostly there was a flood in my mouth

because I wanted to love the toaster
as soon as possible, and the toothbrush
with multilevel bristles
created by dental science, and the walls
holding pictures in front of their faces
to veil the boredom of living

fifty years without once
turning the other way. I wanted
the halo a cheap Beaujolais paints
over everything like artists gave the holy
before perspective was invented,
and for a moment thought in the glow

of fermented bliss that the bending
of spoons by will was inevitable,
just as the dark-skinned would kiss
the light-skinned and those with money
and lakefront homes would open
their verandas and offer trays

of cucumber sandwiches to the poor
scuttling along the fringes of their lawns
looking for holes in the concertina wire.

Of course I had to share this ocean
of acceptance and was soon on the phone
with a woman from Nogales whose hips

had gone steady with mine. I told her
I was over her by pretending I was just
a friend calling to say the snowdrops
had nuzzled through dirt to shake
their bells in April wind. This
threw her off the scent of my anguish

as did the cement mixer of my voice, as did
the long pause during which I memorized
her breathing and stared at my toes
like we were still together, reading
until our eyes slid from the page
and books fell off the bed to pound

their applause as our tongues searched
each other's bodies. When she said
she had to go like a cop telling a bum
to move on, I began drinking downhill,
with speed that grew its own speed,
and fixed on this image with a flagellant's

zeal, how she, returning to bed, cupped
her lover's crotch and whispered not
to worry, it was no one on the phone,
and proved again how forgotten I'd become
while I, bent over the cold confessional,
listened to the night's sole point of honesty.

The bald truth

My hair went on a diet of its own accord.
Rogaine is the extent of my vanity.
It didn't work but it was fun
treating my head with fertilizer
as if it were a phrenologist's lawn.
They were onto something in believing
the skull you have is the soul you are,
that the brain is involved in the sport
of tectonics. My skull has a fault line
like California's, which makes sense
given how the hemispheres of my brain
collide: the right side wants
to clean the house while the left
knows dancing is the best part
of who we are. Or vice versa,
I always have to look that up.
They say baldness means energetic things
about parts of me that aren't
falling off. The real compensation's
having no choice meeting the mirror
but to accept that tomorrow
will be different than today.
And greeting my wife,
not wondering, as pretty men must,
if I'm kissed for my soul or face,
to never doubt, as I become invisible,
that I'm seen by love.

After working sixty hours again for what reason

The best job I had was moving a stone
from one side of the road to the other.
This required a permit which required
a bribe. The bribe took all my salary.
Yet because I hadn't finished the job
I had no salary, and to pay the bribe
I took a job moving the stone
the other way. Because the official
wanted his bribe, he gave me a permit
for the second job. When I pointed out
that the work would be best completed
if I did nothing, he complimented
my brain and wrote a letter
to my employer suggesting promotion
on stationery bearing the wings
of a raptor spread in flight
over a mountain smaller than the bird.
My boss, fearing my intelligence,
paid me to sleep on the sofa
and take lunch with the official
who required a bribe to keep anything
from being done. When I told my parents,
they wrote my brother to come home
from university to be slapped
on the back of the head. Dutifully,
he arrived and bowed to receive
his instruction, at which point
sense entered his body and he asked
what I could do by way of a job.
I pointed out there were stones
everywhere trying not to move,

all it took was a little gumption
to be the man who didn't move them.
It was harder to explain the intricacies
of not obtaining a permit to not
do this. Just yesterday he got up
at dawn and shaved, as if the lack
of hair on his face has anything
to do with the appearance of food
on an empty table.

Oath to my former life

It used to be enough to be bigger
in soul by any means,
whether climbing the water tower
drunk or coked or driving
to the frozen lake on mushrooms
to throw up as the ice
breathed my skin in and out.
I can offer no more literal
description of pilgrimage
than seven black pills
and holding my hand
over fire when pain
as the extent of the world
was perfect clarity.
If now my overturned dog
moaning at the wanderings
of my fingers across her teats
and just a beer shared with my wife
as two girls across the street
in t-shirts etch their thoughts
with sparklers into the air
is the life I want of all
possible miracles, I promise
to remember how to roll a joint
while steering with my thighs.
How to stand in one corner
of a room while looking at myself
waving back at me. How to have
a mouth but no brain, to sell oregano
to men with guns, to fall asleep
in the middle of a room

like babies do, with my ass
in the air and face on the floor,
to wake in this posture
with sunlight washing my skin
and go out for coffee and a slower
life. How to say yes like a river
jumping off a cliff.

Spirit ditty of no fax-line dial tone

The telephone company calls and asks what the fuss is.
Betty from the telephone company, who's not concerned
with the particulars of my life. For instance
if I believe in the transubstantiation of Christ
or am gladdened at 7:02 in the morning to repeat
an eighth time why a man wearing a hula skirt of tools
slung low on his hips must a fifth time track mud
across my white kitchen tile to look down at a phone jack.
Up to a work order. Down at a phone jack. Up to a work order.
Over at me. Down at a phone jack. Up to a work order
before announcing the problem I have is not the problem
I have because the problem I have cannot occur
in this universe though possibly in an alternate
universe which is not the responsibility or in any way
the product, child or subsidiary of AT&T. With practice
I've come to respect this moment. One man in jeans,
t-shirt and socks looking across space at a man
with probes and pliers of various inclinations, nothing
being said for five or ten seconds, perhaps I'm still
in pajamas and he has a cleft pallet or is so tall
that gigantism comes to mind but I can't remember
what causes flesh to pile that high, five or ten seconds
of taking in and being taken in by eyes and a brain,
during which I don't build a shotgun from what's at hand,
oatmeal and *National Geographics,* or a taser from hair
caught in the drain and the million volts of frustration
popping through my body. Even though. Even though his face
is an abstract painting called Void. Even though
I'm wondering if my pajama flap is open, placing me
at a postural disadvantage. *Breathe* I say inside my head,
which is where I store thoughts for the winter. *All*

is an illusion I say by disassembling my fists, letting each
finger loose to graze. *Thank you* I say to kill the silence
with my mouth, meaning fuck you, meaning die
you shoulder-shrugging fusion of chipped chromosomes
and pus, meaning enough. That a portal exists in my wall
that even its makers can't govern seems an accurate mirror
of life. Here's the truce I offer: I'll pay whatever's asked
to be left alone. To receive a fax from me stand beside
your mailbox for a week. It will come in what appears
to be an envelope. While waiting for the fax reintroduce
yourself to the sky. It's often blue and will transmit
without fail everything clouds are trying to say to you.

Insomnia diary

At 5 a.m. light
from their living room
sinks fluorescent teeth
into powder dropped
from the grey womb
of clouds already moving
to Cleveland,
pregnant with snowmen.

I'm a voyeur
in the sense that I float
through the window
of a bungalow
as parents take turns
holding the scream
of their son.

I've seen the thorn
of his voice contort
his body. Seen
his mother's lips
form sounds of comfort,
her only medicine.
Seen the man pace
when not holding the child
and the woman pace
when not holding the child
          and both
pace with the child
in their arms,
small miles of asking

their flesh to heal
a stubborn pain.

We've been together
since one a.m.
This is more intimate
than watching sex,
which may be a confession.
This is more personal
than my tongue's
opinion of saffron.
And though it's not
the dream
in which my left hand
leaves
for a better gardener,
in which I stand
above myself and pet
my eyes, wanting
back in,
it suggests the dream:
a feeling
that each life
is separated
from a life,
that each shadow
has ambitions
to cast its own shadow.

Or just now,
how both parents
made a cave
around their child,
reaching across,
reaching through

each other
until there was one
body, and how it felt
wrong to stare, almost
pornographic
to see the hunger
of a soul to encounter
the nearest thing
to itself.

Go Greyhound

A few hours after Des Moines
the toilet overflowed.
This wasn't the adventure it sounds.

I sat with a man whose tattoos
weighed more than I did.
He played Hendrix on mouth guitar.
His Electric Ladyland lips
weren't fast enough
and if pitch and melody
are the rudiments of music,
this was just
memory, a body nostalgic
for the touch of adored sound.

Hope's a smaller thing on a bus.

You hope a forgotten smoke consorts
with lint in the pocket of last
resort, to be upwind
of the human condition, that the baby
sleeps
and when this never happens,
that she cries
with the lullaby meter of the sea.

We were swallowed by rhythm.
The ultra blond
who removed her wig and applied
fresh loops of duct tape
to her skull,

her companion who held a mirror
and popped his dentures
in and out of place,
the boy who cut stuffing
from the seat where his mother
should have been—
there was a little more sleep
in our thoughts,
it was easier to yield.

To what, exactly—
the suspicion that what we watch
watches back,
cornfields that stare at our hands,
downtowns
that hold us in their windows
through the night?

Or faith, strange to feel
in that zoo of manners.

I had drool on my shirt and breath
of the undead, a guy
dropped empty Buds on the floor
like gravity was born
to provide this service,
we were white and black trash
who'd come
in an outhouse on wheels and still

some had grown—
in touching the spirited shirts
on clotheslines,
after watching a sky of starlings
flow like cursive

over wheat—back into creatures
capable of a wish.

As we entered Arizona
I thought I smelled the ocean,
liked the lie of this
and closed my eyes
as shadows
puppeted against my lids.

We brought our failures with us,
their taste, their smell.
But the kid
who threw up in the back
pushed to the window anyway,
opened it
and let the wind clean his face,
screamed something
I couldn't make out
but agreed with
in shape, a sound I recognized
as everything I'd come so far
to give away.

Finally opening the anthology to Kunitz

I found him in the bathroom. Straight off
he said it's as easy to lose perspective
as a shoe. I inferred this from the word
shriven, just as his picture told me
he's a doorknob worn smooth by turnings,
the hands of night that opened him
to himself. Perhaps snow falling
through a beakered sky or the diva groove
of crickets is as pure as our bond,
based solely on metaphor and sly
enjambment. I'll seek no news of him
but verse. When the whale, moon-body
beached, eye of water condemned
by the corrosive sky, was touched
by the poet, there was no hope
it understood that even ravishment
in certain minds becomes a promise.
I think he'd like how we met
and smile at the rustic music
that accompanied his own, and turn
to the window, to the constellation
of roses, and be warmed to know
that wanting only a moment's occupation,
I found so much faith in his lines
that I stayed well beyond, having forgotten
my purpose.

Free-floating anxiety sounds like a pretty balloon

I need a soft day, soft hour, a minute
without edge or the stare of a man
with homicide in his teeth.
Need a cigarette you can smoke
to get in shape, that sucks
tension out while putting
slimmer thighs in your quiver, something
in menthol or better yet a Cajun
gasper, fag, coffin stick
for blackened lungs that puff on
after the fidgeting fit
have blown their gaskets. Need
to jump from 30 stories up & scream
through tumbling of Olympic merit,
to have my heart stop one two three
times faster than the speed of thought
and land on a serial killer
to applause for my good deed & aim.
I can't have a life any longer
that doesn't include recreational hours
under palm fronds with a woman
who speaks fluent ocean, syllables
that begin a thousand miles away
and arrive at my ear
carrying a tall drink and breeze.
I've been here two score and change
and can't remember when a smile
was high fashion. My basic
complaint's that there's too much
speed, mortal combat & voodoo
floating around, that cars

haven't been replaced by pillows
so spontaneous napping can break out,
that my reflex with obituaries
is to think, more chotchkes for me.
Maybe they had it right in kindergarten,
all I need's a time out, to go off
and rant with my little fists
against the dirt, which listens
but refuses to say what it's learned
these bitter years swallowing us.

Tuesday's walk

This was before stars. A thin broth of clouds
out west and our debate over color, if cobalt
or azure was the apt word for sky,
finally we threw our mouths away
when language got in the way of being stunned.
The earth was new and the carnage
small. Squirrels decapitating tulips, red
and yellow heads, too many lawns
had the acne of grubs, overnight
the magnolia had begun to lose faith,
she wondered if trees ever shed flowers
all at once, I said like a woman
taking off her dress, she said no,
like a man taking off his. The reasons
I'd wear a dress all begin with spring,
the smell of honeysuckle tickling the hair
on my legs and to live without underwear
in jeans is an airless coup. On we went,
the same path as any night or nearly,
sometimes we go up a street we usually
go down, fascinating isn't it, but how things
change, the appearance of a phalanx
of gnomes or the assassination
of a mailbox by cherry bomb, and how
they persist, the steadfast shelter
of awnings and the nostalgia
perfume of just mowed grass,
by these threads we're woven to place.
And so we tell the neighborhood our day,
the swing of hips frees tongues
and that night that morning came up,

how a song in a dead man's voice
about finding love made her think
of a friend recently lost
to a failure of blood, of another's
tidy suicide, who slipped a bag
over his head before the gun, most of all
and all day her grandfather, whose body
had so recently given up. In reply
I picked this from my day, after we passed
the girl playing with fragments of Barbie,
head and torso dancing in her hands
to her hum, how I watched a boy
lick sap from a maple, immune to the sky
and traffic, to all thoughts but the world
as candy, he only stopped to spit bark
from his tongue and to check the flavor
of another tree. When later
we found apple blossoms, soon to be fat
in their dominance of the sky, we each
licked the bark and compared the taste
by sharing tongues, and when the white
cloud of poodle came running
with its alarm going off, we refused
from embrace to give ground.

1935

for Lester Hicok

He rode in the back with apples and wind.
Rumor was a blast furnace in Battle Creek

needed to be fed. He followed the scent
of work, rode in the back with an ax

and pig. In Battle Creek he'd stand with fifty
or a thousand men. They'd shuffle and smoke,

some would talk while others hid in their hats.
After a while a man with a clipboard

would ask what he asked and stare as long
as he liked. His nod meant food. He rode

in the back on a coil of chain-link fence.
It was warm, shadows popped up from the fields.

In Battle Creek he'd stand. A man would come,
he'd wear a tie and his socks would match.

A furnace needed to be fed, a roof had to rise
over dirt, a pile of steel wanted to move

somewhere else. The rumor was work.
He rode without waving to the men

in other trucks. A rumor was often a lock
on a door. He followed the scent,

rode in the back with apples and wind,
with the tools of his hands and the shadow

of his head running beside the truck.
It got to Battle Creek before he did.

He found other men, their hats,
their cigarettes. He found that their eyes

didn't want him. The furnace was happy
and fat, it didn't need to be fed. Rumor

was a man in Flint had a place and a thing
that needed to be done. He followed the scent,

stuck out his thumb. This is how
my grandfather lived. In the back with a pig.

American Studies

Pamela Anderson's breasts are examined by 21
mouths. Tony, back from Cancun and hoping

penicillin still cures a vacation, thinks silicone
lures a demographic taught by Erector Sets

and Legos the limits of desire are primarily
structural. Gwendolyn, rolling brown eyes

behind green contacts, suggests Tony's
overlooked the cannibalistic nature of male

erotics, the need to destroy the subject of arousal
in the machine of profit. Professor "Call

me Bill" Morrison taps a pen between his teeth
before asking if it wouldn't be good to ask

why David Hasselhoff's trunks don't reveal "the true
man." Warren says it's homophobia—"men don't like

to face each other's packages," while Lilly, sneaking
physics, runs a finger down the periodic table

to beryllium and makes a note never to discover
what *Baywatch* is. Then non sequitur Duane bleats,

"Why'd she take them out?" injecting a nanosecond
of confusion, a group double take before the hunt's

resumed. Tony's sure Tommy Lee made her do it, that
he was tired of lifting all that weight, while Mary

quotes *Entertainment Tonight,* primary text
for the class, that removing her implants was a matter

of conscience, a role model's remodeling. Finally
Professor Bill brings the question back

to Duane, who shrugs at the clock and says,
"I don't know, I liked them, they bounced."

Sur Coast diary

I stood where the earth turned itself inside out
like a sock at the end of the day,
mottled rock and grey rock, slate and conglomerate,
a place for my feet and a place for my bag,
I watched an island
vibrate with seals and an island
shiver with cormorants,
my mind on the Pacific plate, my soul
on the North American,
I was torn in half with the speed a fingernail
grows,
I heard the jaws of the earth at work,
the mountains rose, the ocean swallowed.
I saw my reflection in the eye of a black-tailed deer,
we stood five feet apart, it stared at me
with the charisma of the dark side of the moon,
I told it my name,
I collected its breath on my humid tongue,
our confusion was the understanding we shared,
the astonished seconds before panic,
before we remembered it was impossible to touch.
I peed against a tree twice as old
as the Magna Carta,
older than steel-hulled ships, than steel itself,
than cities hived with light,
than the Black Plague but not the plague of money,
than flight
but not the waxy confidence of Icarus,
peed against the red meat of the trunk,
peed against the hegemony of indoor plumbing,
peed against the idea that I am flesh, to prove

I am made of steam, to prove
I am good as gold.
I opened my mouth to the shadow of a condor, swallowed
the Pleistocene,
swallowed the memory of the first hominids
for this black pause in the sky,
this shape that flies
without wing beats, scavenging is a dream
of the clouds, death has earned elegance,
in wide spires the ugly head turns,
the long feathers engross the air, of this hunger
there are 157 examples,
when they're gone a noun will disappear,
a sound will leave our throats,
we'd be more attractive parasites
if we could fly.
I found a house a poet built and a tower,
took notes for him, that the makers
of heavier tyrannies have added a fence
and to the fence a warning that *You are required
to clean up after your dog*, Mr. Jeffers
would not want cable
I assured the man stringing wires
among the eucalyptus, he'd ask
why we store our heads in boxes,
why our legislatures are concerned with poodles,
he'd tell me to go out and lick the Pacific,
turn from the beautiful homes
into a wind whose fetch began in China,
to smell the hands on the other side of the world
cleaning carp, cleaning weapons,
I've come here to shout into the pliant machine
of the swell, to grow small, to wake
in the night and retune my breath to this black
lung.

Capital crime

He'd intended a drive to Moonlight Bay. Bag
of Ruffles and grapes, ham sandwiches
for the ride, beer and a joint for later,

for sunlight on water and clanging bells
and other women in swimsuits and tank tops
he'd try not to look at whenever

she turned away, a reflex. He'd decided
one knee if on sand or grass but otherwise
standing or sitting, certainly outdoors

unless rain and if rain then the tent
and not a bar, never a restaurant, people
can't help but stare, what is life if not

TV? Words weren't ready but he'd have time,
seven hours in the car to look over
at her face on the sly or remember

the care she took of his body
and the carpet and the bathroom tile
when bad clams sent fluids

in all directions from every opening
and not just fluids, love is a washcloth
on the forehead. They'd marry.

She'd say yes as the *Far Rockaway*
dreamed across the bay or some other
mirage of a yacht, gulls

would be pulling nails from the air
or otherwise employing hardware
to make their noise, she'd smile and both

cry and later with friends
gathered around the zirconia's small fire,
he'd kiss her nose as he pooh-poohed

tears. But when did gas hit 2.01? His
F-150 gets ten miles per and as he went
for the emergency 50 kept folded

in the last flap of his wallet
he remembered the valve he had to buy
for his compressor and began the math,

subtracted the chips and grapes
but they always had chips and grapes
on road trips, also the beer, the joint

was free from Tony and what else—the camp-
ground fee, one meal in a restaurant,
suntan lotion. It was shaving pennies

that did it, you've got to know this. Sure
he could forget the beer and flip-flops
and make it, she'd not mind that

if she'd never complained about the six
months he was laid off and living
in a trailer park anyway, or that Swanson

Hungry Man dinners passed as a culinary
event, but breathing fumes as he thought
about gas running up a buck

in a couple months, he could read,
the oil guys always whined
how they were hurting for dough

under headlines of record profits, just
like his boss never had enough
for a quarter bump though he tooled

into the lot each year in a new Caddy,
the only question was color, red
or blue, and maybe not the fumes

but they helped, maybe not love but love
is enough, wanting one perfect thing, cheap
but perfect, or just being 37 and having

to forego flip-flops, aren't they
a right, isn't summer made of certain
rituals, at least one day giving the soul

back to water, some beer, a sandwich
and a joint, the chance for wedded
bliss? And no he shouldn't have screamed

at the man behind the counter
who didn't understand him anyway, who
was trained to finger the silent alarm

if threats to the Slim Jims arise, no
he shouldn't have tried to explain
to the cops, they have no sympathy

for run-on sentences, pepper spray
is how they argue economic theory,
a poor man can't afford two minutes

of his life unhinged, to resemble
an exploded-view drawing of a bicycle
with too much assembly required. That

she said yes outside the station
after posting bail led to a night
of impossible tumbling and a long,

naked conversation on the picnic table
under a sheet and stars until sunlight
and the embarrassment of neighbors'

hoots. Happiness is the technical term
for what ensued, a week of touching
and talking and sweeping the floors

together and how wonderful it can be
to take out the trash, the only weight
he felt were his socks, without them

he'd have floated off, he almost believed
this was the feeling he'd carry
to his grave, that lips and fingerprints

are wealth. But then he took
the corner at Maple and Wallace slowly,
enjoying the sway and the sound

of a bag of charcoal sliding in the bed
of his truck, when the numbers
on the Sunoco board came clear, $2.19

for unleaded, and the little man
with the branding iron went to work
behind his eyes, the burn that comes

when you're old enough to know
that of all you could hope your most
insane wish is just to be flush.

Now and then I am direct

It's late and I've stayed up to miss you.
A man on TV's playing lute with dirty fingernails.
I hear a car and understand
it would be more useful if taught to fetch.
I want hot chocolate. I want to remember
the first time I heard music and knew
I was hearing music, and the first time
I heard music and had no idea what it was.
I don't ever want to use the word *hype* again.
I'm also trying to be, if not a cup half full,
at least not a cup smashed into a thousand pieces
on the floor kind of person. When I'm tired
it's easier to believe things could be worse.
I'm grateful we have a shopping list
for starters, a simple ode to bread, to milk.
That I have a mind which assumes a man
with dirty fingernails works with wood.
It occurs to me I could be standing in line
one day with money and completely forget
what it's for. The woman behind me
would explain but in the explaining
begin to laugh. I was in Athens and people
were shooting up along the path
to the Acropolis. This was not beautiful,
not Greek. There was sex in the bushes
that made flesh sound like a calamity of gears.
But at the top a woman was explaining Nike
to her daughter, who only cared to know
where our wings went. Don't repeat that,
it could become a t-shirt. I'm worried our bed
can't sleep without us. When you come back,

if the spoons are missing, would you look
in the backyard to see if I've built a river?
I haven't, but a boat. Not a boat but a sail.
At least the cloth. At least the wind
on which the sail feeds.

Growing at the speed of fashion

for A.

It gets harder to find untroubled ways
to feel beautiful with so
many nipples selling beer on TV.

She's eight and convinced her skin's
an insult to the cotton weaves
and rayons called clothes.

Her hips alone are schizophrenic,
too wee for the wiggle
she wants
though she's also convinced
they could be smaller, more
ambiance than support.

I remember things about eight
that might be relevant here
like not remembering anything about eight.

I've seen pictures. I had
exploding hair and must have loved
the earth because I wore dirt
to every occasion.

Hiding should be the career of a child.
Breaking things
is good or licking rocks.

Her ears are pierced, she likes
to pull rouge from a plastic purse
and brag it across her cheeks.

Just alone in a corner of the couch
with a book and chewing her hair
she's gorgeous like air
and water are to delirious flesh.

When we were fish, cool
wasn't a problem, gangly girls
on the savannah didn't ask
what implants are.

She giggles when her mother says
balloons and runs
outside, hair dancing back
like wheat in a storm.

To sandbox, swings, to pester the dog
from its siesta?

No, there's a patch she's worn
to dirt honing the reflex
of catwalk.

Beside the swing set, under the willow's
dreadlocks, she tries to fit
inside the glide she's seen
models own
but stumbles
more than floats, her dream defeated
by her bones.

And the pause before the turn
she gets wrong, her habit's
still the sleepy pace
of show and tell,
but with reps she'll improve,

she has the drive
that comes from knowing
she's nothing if not watched.

Bars poetica

This is the story I've tried to tell. Guy
exists. Father mother sister brother.
Oh pretty stars, oh bastard moon
I see you watching me. The trembling
years leading to sex, the trembling sex.
Death as garnish. Death as male lead,
female lead, death as a cast
of thousands. God in, on, as, with,
to, around, because who knows
because. All the while feeling air's
a quilt of tongues, that spaces
between words are more articulate
than words. It's not like you'd hope,
that anyone can make sense.
Look around you, let your ears
breathe deep—almost no one does.
Have another drink. When they throw us out
there's a place down the street
that never closes, and when it does
we'll climb a fire escape and praise
the genealogy of light. The Big Bang
sounds like what it was, the fucking
that got everything under way.
That love was there from the start
is all I've been trying to say.

Translator's note

There is a tradition in Laparona that the first
man to wake each morning must sweep
shadows from his porch lest night
pull the long limbs of sunlight
into its mouth and devour the day.
Serto wants to be the broom melting dark
and light in the moment of their divorce.
This teases the translator with a feast
of moral and technical difficulties. For
example. There is a widely chattered rumor
that the arm Serto lost in the last battle
for Muipo, now passed by Zedefi rebels
from base to base in the Chimasta mountains,
reverts to his body in dream and chokes him
to death, his last breath the word *benudok*.
In Kuntolo this means something like traitor/
savior. The aspiration, for which there is no
simple English equivalent, in fact no
comparable word in the Romance "pallet,"
is to hold in one unit of language the complex
idea of the man or woman who saves a village
or clan by a putatively faithless act,
the virtue of which only he or she is aware.
In the first sentence of *Kiloso dak Vermoso* or
Swallowed River, Serto injects the legend
of his missing arm into our imaginations
in words of necessary misinterpretation. *Ekiu zar
sedru dok erchulo tubuso* can be translated one
of two ways—*The arm rose and embraced the sun*
or *The arm rose and devoured the sun*. Given
Serto's standing as a world writer,

the opening sentence is a challenge
to translators to base the tone of the novel
on the seesaw of a single word. By the time
Mersatta, tortured by the dream of the arm,
hangs himself from the 300-year-old
kloson tree in the square of his unnamed village,
it is clear the arm has been the novel's
narrator, and that if *erchulo* had been translated
as embraced, Mersatta is to be forgiven,
as devoured, Mersatta should be left to rot.
Further complicating matters is that sometimes
the narrator is the arm but others a tongue
or foot, there is an entire chapter called
Bukosaman or Metronome, where the narrator
becomes, without reference until the last word
of the chapter, the gold buckle of General
Cuntare's belt. As always with Serto, we are made
to wonder, knowing so much about his life—
the shuttling of rebel messages as a child
along the honed ridges of the Chimastas,
the rape of his mother, shooting of his father
before his eyes, the sudden appearance
of a wealthy uncle who shipped the boy
out of the country into the arms of the Treost
Jesuits, his return as the lunatic pen
behind the incendiary pages of *The Undressed
Land*—if we are not being asked to wear
the complexity of his guilt and decide if he,
the supposed informer at Muipo, is a child
of reverence or scorn. Out of this tempest
I have essentially written my own book. Mersatta
still dies but is happy to let the sway
of his body replace the wind's tick-tock.
The arm which haunts him has nothing to say
about the revolution but wants to come home.

At the end the two are reconciled into a single
body of death. After that the country is quiet,
rebels come down from the mountains
to discover their families have long ago left,
packed rivers and wheat fields and nailed
a note to the barbershop saying *Don't follow,*
after twenty years your eyes can no longer see
our skin. Then the rebels take the mountains apart,
I leave them with mouths full of dirt, hands
clawed to nubs in bereavement, and Serto
in the distance in the guise of the Guitano,
a sea famed for placid waters but hiding
the Judas teeth of rocks.

Echo

He or she let go of my wife and me.
The doctor said *it*, stressing objectivity.
Blood on denim looks like water at first.
Water interprets wind subjectively.

The child returned its face to the wind.
If I repeat myself I should say something new.
The doctor's smile was a weak cup of tea.
Blood on tile's a form of clarity.

When I say something new I repeat myself.
A child would repeat and erase ourselves.
We had a list of names, column girl, column boy.
We waited for the face to decide itself.

She stood in the door with blood on her jeans.
I was reading a book I won't read again.
My wife thinks her genes let go of the child.
The doctor said no, stressing his certainty.

The nurse almost tiptoed around the room.
Wind takes a broom to water, repeating its name.
My wife and I slept awake in different rooms.
We each let go and have never explained.

It's hard to prove by flesh you give no blame.
Blood unlike water never truly goes away.
Each name carried a different clarity.
We repeat to each other *it's impossible to explain.*

The doctor hoped we would try again.
When we touch she moves like water under wind.
In her flesh I hear the names repeat themselves.
Blood on her hands will never be new.

It's impossible to stop wanting to repeat ourselves.
We slept in different rooms with our shame.
It's impossible to bury names under wind.
Blood dissolves in water without blame.

Mortal shower

I met my butt in a Pittsburgh
hotel room. My face
still looks like my face
but not my butt, my hair

no longer resembles an ad
for Jell-O pudding, people thought
it was chocolate pudding for years,
so thick

and rich. There was fog
in the bathroom and then not fog,
I faced my face
and then not my face, the mirror

staring at my ass
winked at the mirror
staring at my face

and the future was defined
as an effort
to use the word sag in my resume.
Have sagged, will

sag, am looking for a position
in which to maximize my sagging
potential. I once cared
what went on back there, about

the extent of grip and rise, just
as some birds crave

the reddest plumage, and I propositioned
mirrors, watched women's eyes
follow, turned in shop windows
to see if my pants
fit their purpose. Then love

and car payments, love and the sofa
needs to be moved, love and her grandmother
dies, my grandmother
dies, love
and she comes home and I'm thrilled
by her coat and voice
and the brown habit of her eyes. She

likes my ass and lies
about its travels, how it's lost
focus, and there are wattles
to come, please God
if dentures
only partials, may Depends

be cheap in bulk and the earth
generous with its telepathy, I'm

in Pittsburgh tonight
                                    and with her,
mirrors don't scare me,
room service is a gas
because she's alive, I'm a giant,
a tight-assed
titan because she's alive
and says

            come home, the Honda needs
new brakes, a robin flew

into the window today
but shook it off, just
dizzy, stunned
by reflection.

Meteor shower

It's the one shower I take each year.
Naked in the field with skeletons
of corn. Water's got fresh skin
but crack it open and there's filth,
the sundry goos we've given away
coming home to lick us.
To get clean you need something
out of this world. But what sadness
pushes stars to suicide? In truth
they're rocks, we call them stars
to speak kindly of the dead.
When they fall nearby I hear a fizz
that makes me think the universe
is made of champagne. If you wash
with light you rinse with air,
it's good for the complexion.
Real stars are the womb of everything,
pebbles and the bright logos
of tropical fish. If naked
in a field I ask the long-legged
corn to dance, a twirl is certain.
Who can resist this hot music,
these ballroom lights?

Building a painting a home

If I built a barn I'd build it right into the sky

with windows twice as large as walls and ringed
with theoretical pines, clumps of green on simple sticks

and doors cut from the ocean, doors that wave
and doors that foam and shadows inside to eat

every cow I own because I'm afraid of cows,
four stomachs imply that aliens are involved,

moo is what the brainwashed say, my fields
would be green until yellow and yellow

until white, acres of albino wheat
for the manufacture of weightless bread,

I only eat what floats in a house that spins
as the weather vane turns, a house that follows

a rooster in love with wind, the sky
and my barn are blue and the sky also floats,

there's nothing to hold anything down,
even eternity's loose and roams the erotic

contortions of space, even my children
recognize tomorrow better than they remember

today, if I built a barn I'd build the land
and the sun before that, I'd spread the canvas flat

with my hands and nail it to the dirt, I'd paint
exactly what I see and then paint

over that until by accident something habitable
appears, until the kettle screams on the stove,

until the steam is green and the sound is gold.

Commission by attrition

Who's to say gravity isn't love? The landing
was gracious, my jigsaw body

intact but with all
the honey-roasted peanuts I could fit
in my pockets and this

is embrace. This
is 10,000 gallons of fuel to fly
from one
rental car to another, white
Saturn, blue Sable, here clouds

resemble Mickey Mantle at the plate, there
Mick at the bar
with highball. Imagine mountains

colonizing the sky or river
slinking off, the crenellated
cityscape,
picture I-54321
blastoff, someone's

Fed-Exed my hotel room, it arrives
before me, premonition of comfy
mattress, window

facing fire escape, local news
begins symphonic, ends with a puppy
called Redemption.

                    I tell
the story of gaskets, there's drama
in valves, what
they let in, keep out, and if you don't have
filters, if air's
just what it is and not

what you tell it to be, if the little
bones, the knives
aren't removed from water before it enters
your Amber's mouth,

she might not reach the prom, can I put you down
for a million, I'll pop
for freight if you buy the next round. Who's

to say my body isn't
sacrifice, burger burger burger, what's
a colon
after all but temporary, some
blood in the stool, some

insomnia for my Amy, Todd
who just discovered his voice
is heroin to his mother, I come here

and here is not here, there's no place
I ever am
and this is falling, who's to say

love isn't a power suit, Power
Book, coffee
for breakfast
lunch
dinner coffee

for the hollow bones, I'm falling
into your life

with brochures, will you catch

my arrhythmia, take my calls,
buy
one more ball-valve with neoprene
seat
than you'll ever need, my soul's

at the airport, my body
was sent to Dallas,

I gave up luggage for Lent and carry
my toothbrush in my useless
chest.

Goodbye in the shape of a knot

I am stuck. Everything I want to say
about the flowers massing for attack, black-eyed
Susans and something blue and frilly,
about my mother's gallbladder
sitting lonely in the surgical tray,
about the hum of frogs over my head
at night when I walk the familiar loop
so my dog can sniff the urine-text
of grass, turns to my obsession
with the kids of Smolensk who used
frozen German corpses as sleds
during World War II because they had
snow and nothing else. Step one
is to admit I have a problem. Or,
to read the Keith Jarrett interview
in *Utne Reader* sideways, across
the columns of his thoughts, "Keep going
somewhere. And microdetail. This
is actually that's what I do. I find
a way the only way someone can
to get off the earth, and as do this
and get away with it. I work my way up—
as the if you're going to get music
is being played—I am burned
by flame, you very aware. I have prepared
don't just wander around my awareness." Mean
to show from my head the happiness
of dark things—to have a body
under you very fast or with
empty stomach and bombs say going off
in your mother's hair, to laugh

down a hill and drag back up
the stiff, to make wind in your teeth
of death. Because you are
is why I bother, dying and better
than me, faster to the point of soon
doctors say, make a promise to you
of my obsession, this comfort you must
think sideways to feel. That
when you're gone I'll use your life
to good ends, be the first
to jump on your grave and admit
there was no everything
other than love to call it
ecstasy, or aiming this arrow
at living and breathing, at the event
I'm divorcing the same moment
it happens, call your face to others
as a shape to live within, your smile
a quest for the pure
improvisation of things.

The edge

One day the kid showed up with a tattoo of a stapler
on his shoulder. The others had tattoos of geckoes
and fish and the Incredible Hulk, an emerald
Lou Ferrigno against a background of fire. He'd
have been beaten up except they were dazed by it,
not just the precise cursive of the word *Swingline*
or the luster of the striking plate but the fact
of the stapler itself. He got the last pizza
at lunch and was touched on the wrist by a girl
at the fountain. This made him believe he was real
in a way breathing never had. Over the next
few months he stopped feeling he lived
on the wrong side of the mirror. There
was an election & his name was penciled in
on a few ballots. The guy with the red Camaro
gave him a ride home and let him pick the music.
In second-period French he stood to ask
what Harcourt Brace knew all men wanted to know,
if Monique and Evette would join him Saturday
on the sailboat. First the teacher cried,
then the students sang the Marseillaise
because in four years all he'd ever said
was *comment allez-vous?* No one questioned the tattoo.
Who'd believe he got up to pee and it was there,
just as the image of the body of Christ
appeared one morning on the thigh
of St. Barthelme of Flours. Otherwise
their stories differ. St. Barthelme was stoned
to death. The kid went to homecoming in a tux
with blue cumulus cuffs and a girl
embarrassed by anything but the slowest dance.

Radical neck

A match beaten by frail wind lights the cave
of his hands, lines that jump like the ibex
of Cosquer in the rippling glow of a torch,
the hunting-magic of vanished men. Smoke
weaves through his lungs into blood, ghost
of plants, of the earth returning to his body.
One Camel down, nineteen to go. Another image:
on the train to St. Louis when windows still
opened: when men wore hats like boys now aspire
to tattoos: one hand on his hip, the other
swinging a smoke back and forth, a small
rhythm falling inside the generous rhythm
of the train. He turned and smiled at my mother,
pointed to a red barn falling down, being
absorbed by the horizon. He stood almost
the whole way, giving his glance to the distance,
and returned to our seats larger, puffed
as if he'd become part of land's green wish.

_____

"The skull had a tongue in it, and could sing
once."

_____

Always the question of how to address the dead.
Dear sir. Beloved though rotted man. You

who dwell in the scented couch, fabric of walls.
Yet my father remains exact in what he says,

each communiqué encoded in action, something
he did, as if he returns through what I recall.

Visitations, translucent frames, his arms arcing
toward a block of wood, the ax bold in appetite:

the bow his hands made tying shoes, always left
then right, a celestial order: wrist-snap of Zippo

top, the crisp click into place like the settling
of doubt, his fingerprints on the metal case

proof he'd mastered the prophecy of fire. His
advantage: forever happy in these things:

or precisely morose: or bent toward a river's
"slow and mileconsuming clatter" with a face

washed of need or edge, the only moment I saw him
absolved of himself. A crystal will only form

around a speck, an imperfection: in a rush a world
arises, encloses, becomes. Like this he comforts,

intrudes, a twin voice in a restaurant invokes his face,
then slides his laugh and fetid breath into place,

and for a second nothing lives that isn't him:
I've no recourse but to pursue: yet he's done with me.

———

Radical
neck:
dissection and removal of jaw, lymph nodes, tongue.

At the VA they called them half-heads, chop-blocks.

I visited intending to stare like a child,
to covet his words, by then muted by phlegm,
the esophageal churnings of an aborted throat.

But I looked in bursts, seconds before I'd turn
to Williams Pond or the far copse of alders,
hoping wind was caught in the water, in the hair
of trees, that robin or rose would hover as excuse,
a glory requiring my eyes.

No one came close, even staff strayed until
it was time to wheel him in.

All the while he smoked, plumes escaping the tube,
all love given that pursuit, a reflex gone deeper
than life.

———

As a child I loved the smoke because it adored him, clung
to, stroked his face, filled the Valiant with an animal
made of endless shapes. And the packs themselves, smell
of tobacco new, unlit, the music Raleigh, Chesterfield,
Lark, ashtrays shaped as Buddhas, crowns and spaceships.
The cough was always there, his second voice, and when
wasn't someone asking him to stop, my mother, then me,
then doctors holding his clubbed fingers, explaining
a man shouldn't pass out getting dressed. The smoke clung,
became his skin. When asked what I wanted done I said
burn him, make him ash: my revenge: his only wish.

It's not so much the heat as the stupidity

Excuse me but I'd like to say something that should
in no way be taken as representing other things
I might say or words I could put down
on paper but haven't. And if you extrapolate
from my remarks to other remarks you've heard
or made yourself about the proper use of
or protection of resources from certain uses
then you'll think I speak for a cause or against
that cause with the kind of vehemence
that has spittle flying through the air
and onto your nose and there you are, wanting
to be polite but needing desperately
to wipe it away. It's just that I don't mind
really or take it as a danger to my dog
or children or car or the crackers I have
which are admittedly stale but still a comfort
in the pantry that I paid for with hard work
because and I apologize for this in advance
and mean no slight to the political affiliation
of your god or the fondness you have
for a clear green space at night you can imagine
never walking through but of course trees
need their alone time too and here I'll apologize
once more if it's untoward to say that on a night
such as this when the axis of the earth
has tilted away from the sun and the great
comfort of a quilt lies at your feet
or over your feet and the dragon in your basement
snorts hot breath into your house that I don't
mind if people sleep on the grates in the park
over steam that's going to heaven anyway because
otherwise and I know it's rude to mention this
they'll die.

Cure for the common cold

I was having an affair with fever as winter
dreamed its first snow, as trees became old men
in unbuttoned long johns, as wind
locked its face in the river's ice.

Under seven blankets I invented July.

Daylilies grew from my underarms.
My head was a field
grasshoppers mowed with lyrical scythes.
In each eye was a lake, in each lake
a man in a rowboat
read *Moby Dick* to trout to make them brave.

When the fever broke and I opened
the gaze of the curtains,
I thought I'd parachuted into another mind.

I was in Andy Hardy's swimsuit.
I was chewing grape hyacinth.
But instead of a beer in my hand
I needed a shovel.
Instead of a tan
it was time for January's
albino camouflage.

I wanted back into the fever,
its red walls,
the lush carpet from the Everglades.

I was happier sweating
because it proves the body's made of rain.
I was happier hallucinating a beach

because I'm a better man
in the presence of a water slide.
I was happier when my flesh
was a sauna because I could run
like a naked Swede
through cow-shaped hills
and burn away the snow with my thighs.

People would see my brand on the earth,
the singed and fat signature
of my existence.

They'd go off in search of their own
fevers,
kissing the maps of tongues,
licking the dirty maze of fingertips.

Winter is always rape, a curse
against our hunger, because we starve
for seven pomegranate seeds.

Proserpina got this much right:
be the best at picking blossoms:
be the best at tasting where rivers sleep in rock:
be the best at harboring a thaw in your body,

lips and thighs that will open to the sun,
skin you can peel and throw into the mouth
of the sky like a monarch you made from scratch.

Cutting edge

I can't be in the avant-garde
because I cry when dogs die

in movies. Worse, I sniffle
if they're abandoned or hit

with even the rolled and tepid
discipline of *Newsweek*. My dog

is eight. When I do the math
I get weepy. I see the hole

in the backyard I'll dig,
pet her while imagining

how I'll pet her as the vet
slips the needle in. During

these moments she licks tears
and snot from my face, just

as she took menstrual blood
from my wife's finger

this morning for what it is.
Anyway, sorrow about a dog

looks silly in a beret. It
should be plainspoken,

like everything else
I try hard not to say.

Truth about love

I apologize for not being Gandhi or Tom
      the mailman who is always kind.

He makes his way every day no matter
      the mood of the sky with our words

in a sack and Gandhi made the English
      give India back without

taking a gun for a wife. My contribution
      to the common good is playing

with the alphabet in a little room
      while the world goes foraging

for food. I'm a better poet than man
      and it's well known how little

my verbs are worth. I am my only subject,
      being the god of my horizons.

What saves me is that just beyond my skin
      the world of yours is where

I'd rather live. The AMA says you've added
      seven point six years to my life.

In a phrase, love is a transfer of wealth.
      This is why Adam Smith gave up

romantic verse. In trying to say what can't
      be said I'll take the *Dragnet*

approach. Just the facts. I'd be dead
      sooner without you, you'll die faster

for being a Mrs., raw deal can't be more
      clearly defined. To make amends

I offer ten percent more kisses each year.
      Or do I do more harm the closer

we become? If yes, leaving would be love
      and a better man might. But my thrills

are selfishly domestic. I like sweeping words
      into piles and whispering *good night.*

Shopping at the ocean

Trying to save the bug she killed the bug
and I won't call you dumb ass by saying
there's a lesson in this. There was a smear
in this and driving and some music
from our past that captured our hands
and heads with its embarrassing sweetness.
We were traveling toward shoes or spoons
or rice in white boxes, always we are buying
something, I haven't made anything useful
since I filled construction paper
with a red sky and green sun
and then unrolled my body into a nap. She
was talking and fortunately I watched
her lips form sounds about a grandfather
who shouldn't be alone because the lips
revealed a quaver hidden by the folds
of the sounds, her face needed to cry
while her voice pretended
it was in the next room asking
if I want tea. She's like this
more than anyone should be like this,
wanting to help her grandfather
wrestle with food and air and the suddenly
spidery nature of sheets, at 87
everything's a tangle and driving
to buy soap or corn chips she remembers
that making change last Tuesday for a paper
he blanked on quarter and dime and just
opened his palm and let the man
wade through the silver waters.
I won't call you idiot by saying emotions

are like plate tectonics but her chin
buckles to the upwelling fear and what
she can't change she fastens on with greatest
devotion. Now and then someone will live
forever but otherwise the trajectories
are fixed. She knows this and that the bug
she tried to scoot out the window
had seven hours to live before a bat
scooped up another pinging meal.
There's no possible segue to the romance
we'd intended our lives to contain. I'm
a dumb ass because what I offer
for comfort is straight off the shelf, hand
on the thigh, kiss on the cheek, I excel
at purring *uh-huh* in a way that drives
the speaker on toward exhaustion. For her
I'd be a poison eater, my mouth
divine, I'd suck the sorrow out and spit
its thrashing body from the window
and there, her grandfather would live
forever, there, her friend's father
would rip the cancer from his chest
and weave it into a basket, there, she and I
will see mountains get bored
with clouds and money turn
to swallowtails and the moon
split into seven moons so there's always
one in the sky when you drive
to the ocean instead of the store
and get out of the car and swear
at emptiness because you know it's the animal
that will win.

Acknowledgments

I'd like to thank the editors of the following publications for reading my crap and everyone's crap yet remaining determined and (somewhat) sane: *Boulevard, Chelsea, Conduit, Iowa Review, The Journal, Michigan Quarterly Review, Mid-American Review, Missouri Review, New England Review, Poetry Flash, Poetry Northwest, Prairie Schooner, Shenandoah, The Southeast Review, The Southern Review,* and *Witness.*

"Cure for the common cold" and "Growing at the speed of fashion" first appeared in the *American Poetry Review.*

"An old story" first appeared in the *New Yorker.*

"Radical neck" first appeared in *TriQuarterly,* a publication of Northwestern University.

"Becoming bird" was reprinted in *Dorothy Parker's Elbow* (Warner, 2002) and *The Year's Best Fantasy and Horror* (St. Martin's, 2002)

"Bottom of the ocean" and "Radical neck" were reprinted in *Contemporary American Poetry: Behind the Scenes* (Longman, 2003)

"Building a painting a home" was reprinted in *Pushcart XXIV* and *New Poems from the Third Coast* (Wayne State University Press, 2000)

"Echo" was reprinted in *Poets of the New Century* (Godine, 2001)

"Echo," "The edge," "Growing at the speed of fashion," "The semantics of flowers on Memorial Day," and "Small purchase" appeared on *Poetry Daily.*

BOB HICOK is the author of *Animal Soul* (2001), which was a finalist for the National Book Critics Circle Award, *Plus Shipping* (1998), and *The Legend of Light* (1995), which won the 1995 Felix Pollak Prize in Poetry and was named a 1997 ALA Booklist Notable Book of the Year. A recipient of two Pushcart Prizes and an NEA Fellowship, he has been published in numerous literary journals and anthologies, including the 1997 and 1999 volumes of *Best American Poetry*. Having owned a successful die design business, he is currently an assistant professor of English at Virginia Tech in Blacksburg.